A Child's Treasury of NURSERY RHYMES

A Child's Treasury of NURSERY RHYMES

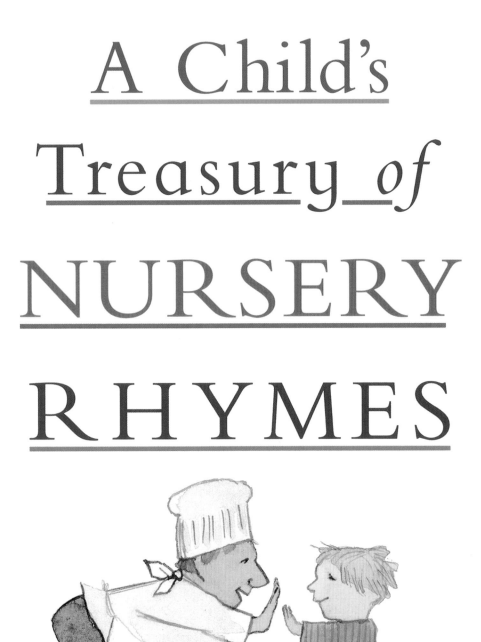

~ Kady MacDonald Denton ~

Kids Can Press

Published by arrangement with Kingfisher Publications Plc

This selection © 1998 Kady MacDonald Denton
Illustrations © 1998 Kady MacDonald Denton
The moral right of the illustrator has been asserted.

Kids Can Press Ltd.
29 Birch Avenue
Toronto, ON M4V 1E2

www.kidscanpress.com

Designed by Rebecca Elgar

Printed and bound in Canada

CDN 98 0 9 8 7 6 5 4 3
CDN PA 02 0 9 8 7 6 5 4 3 2 1

National Library of Canada Cataloguing in Publication Data

Main entry under title:
A child's treasury of nursery rhymes

Includes index.
ISBN 1-55074-554-9 (bound).   ISBN 1-55337-512-2 (pbk.)

1. Nursery rhymes, English. I. Denton, Kady MacDonald

PZ8.3.C53 1998   j398.8   C98-930859-6

Kids Can Press is a *lorus*™ Entertainment company

CONTENTS

INTRODUCTION

To be asked to illustrate a collection of nursery rhymes and to make the selection made me feel like a kid in a candystore! I began with rhymes that delighted me as a child and have stayed with me through the years. I added rhymes loved by my children and some classic favourites. I found rhymes that were new to me, from as far afield as China, Africa and India: little gems that made me laugh and reminded me that everywhere babies cry, parents soothe and children want to play.

Slowly this treasury took shape. There were rhymes to sing, whisper, shout and twist the tongue around; toe-tapping phrases that spin off images as fast as a pin-wheel. What magic for a child! What a delight for an illustrator! I wanted to catch those images I saw spinning from the rhymes; to please those who read pictures and not words by telling my own visual stories. But the broad range of the verses needed a structure. I cleared the floor and covered it with little pieces of paper, trying to sort the verses into some kind of order. They naturally split into four piles: rhymes about the things in a baby's world; the traditional rhymes of Mother Goose which toddlers so love; and anything that reminded me of chalk and wet wool socks went into a pile for a schoolchild. That left a fourth pile full of songs, dashing pieces and bits of fun that *everyone* enjoys. Thus this collection is split into four sections, designed to appeal to children at different stages in their lives. But of course, the engaging rhythms and irrepressible language of all the rhymes can be enjoyed at *any* age.

The first section is about babies. I remember as a new parent being thrilled to discover that rhyme will amuse and comfort a tiny child. The section begins with some familiar verses of discovery (*eye winky, mouth merry*) because one of the very first things we do when faced with a newborn is to study the little package. There are bouncing rhymes and rhymes to cheer the events of baby's day: mealtime (*Sippity sup, sippity sup*), playtime (*Pat a cake, pat a cake*) and bedtime (*Rock-a-bye baby*). Lullabies, of course, belong in this section as they are among the most beautiful and evocative

of all nursery verse. And because we fall in love with babies, I have included *Lavender's Blue* and *My Luve is Like a Red, Red Rose.*

The second section follows the pattern of a toddler's day – up, eat, out, play, walk, supper, bath and bed – simple events celebrated in songs that encourage playfulness and suggest action. Here are the classics of the world of Mother Goose. We meet Georgie Porgie and the girl with the curl right in the middle of her forehead. I never liked Little Miss Muffet and was happy to discover the more spirited Little Miss Tuckett, so here she is. Most of these poems are short. They are easy to remember. We *do* remember them. Their curious characters delight us still.

The third section reflects the energy of young schoolchildren with playground chants, verses and nonsense pieces. Here is rollicking out-loud language with rhythms like drumbeats. Perhaps *A was an Apple Pie* was composed by a schoolchild wishing for lunch. I don't know. Many nursery rhymes have unknown origins. But it is a lovely mix of images to which I have added an animal puzzle. The mischievious ditty about no more school has such appeal for schoolchildren everywhere that one version, from the Caribbean, was an irresistible choice to end this section.

The fourth section is full of the things that older children will enjoy, set within the world of an old-fashioned fair. The excitement is familiar even if it is experienced more often now at a holiday family celebration or a street parade. It is a gathering of all ages and generations. Here are verses to have fun with and to share with everyone – sing-along songs, nonsense rhymes, riddles, tongue-twisters and limericks. (*Skip To My Lou* lends itself to all sorts of invented additional lines.) Many of the old rhymes tell of courtship and love, and since these seem to fascinate children, a few are also included.

As a child I loved Edward Lear's enchanting *The Owl and the Pussy-Cat,* and I chose it to close this collection. We can all share favourite verses with a child and so rediscover the joyful spirit of nursery rhyme. In that world, we all dance to the light of the moon.

Kady MacDonald Denton

Manitoba, 1998

For the children now who will grow up
in the 21st century.

Welcome, Little Baby

D ance, little Baby, dance up high!
Never mind, Baby, Mother is by.
Crow and caper, caper and crow,
There, little Baby, there you go!

Baby Face,
    You've got the cutest little Baby Face,
There's not another one could take your place.
Baby Face,
My poor heart is jumpin',
You sure have started somethin',
Baby Face;
I'm up in heaven when I'm in your fond embrace,
I didn't need a shove
'Cause I just fell in love with your pretty Baby Face.

Harry Akst and Benny Davis

Brow brinky,
   Eye winky,
Chin choppy,
Cheek cherry,
Mouth merry.

Clap hands for mama till papa come!
   Bring cake and sugar-plum,
    And give baby some!

Round and round the garden
   Like a teddy bear,
One step,
Two steps,
Tickly under there.

11

Curly-locks, Curly-locks, wilt thou be mine?
Thou shalt not wash dishes, nor yet feed the swine;
But sit on a cushion, and sew a fine seam
And feed upon strawberries, sugar and cream.

Jerry Hall
He is so small,
A rat could eat him,
Hat and all.

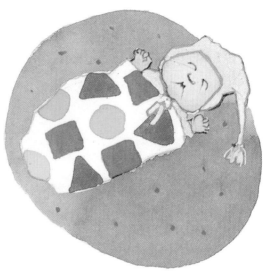

Polly, Dolly, Kate and Molly,
Are all filled with pride and folly.
Polly tattles, Dolly wriggles,
Katy rattles, Molly giggles;
Whoever knew such constant rattling,
Wriggling, giggling, noise and tattling.

This little cow eats grass,
　　This little cow eats hay,
This little cow drinks water,
This little cow runs away,
And this little cow does nothing
But lie down all the day.

Moses supposes his toeses are roses,
　　But Moses supposes erroneously;
For nobody's toeses are posies of roses
As Moses supposes his toeses to be.

Shoe a little horse,
　　Shoe a little mare,
　　But let the little colt
　　Go bare, bare, bare.

This is the way the ladies ride,
Tri, tre, tre, tree,
Tri, tre, tre, tree;
This is the way the ladies ride,
Tri, tre, tre, tre, tri-tre-tre-tree!

This is the way the gentlemen ride,
Gallop-a-trip,
Gallop-a-trot;
This is the way the gentlemen ride,
Gallop-a-gallop-a-trot!

This is the way the farmers ride,
Hobbledy-hoy,
Hobbledy-hoy;
This is the way the farmers ride,
Hobbledy, hobbledy-hoy!

14

F ather and Mother and Uncle John
Went to market one by one.
Father fell off!
Mother fell off!
But Uncle John went on and on,
And on and on and on . . . *and on . . . . and on . . . . and on . . .*

Three little kittens
    They lost their mittens,
  And they began to cry,
Oh, Mother dear,
We sadly fear,
    Our mittens we have lost.
What! Lost your mittens,
You naughty kittens!
      Then you shall have no pie.
      Me-ow, me-ow, me-ow.
      No, you shall have no pie.

The three little kittens
They found their mittens,
    And they began to cry,
Oh, Mother dear,
See here, see here,
    Our mittens we have found.
Put on your mittens,
You silly kittens,
    And you shall have some pie.
    Purr-r, purr-r, purr-r,
    Oh, let us have some pie.

The three little kittens
Put on their mittens,
    And soon ate up the pie,
Oh, Mother dear,
We greatly fear,
    Our mittens we have soiled.
What! Soiled your mittens,
You naughty kittens!
    Then they began to sigh,
    Me-ow, me-ow, me-ow,
    Then they began to sigh.

The three little kittens
They washed their mittens,
    And hung them out to dry,
Oh, Mother dear,
Do you not hear,
    Our mittens we have washed.
What! Washed your mittens,
Then you're good kittens,
    But I smell a rat close by.
    Me-ow, me-ow, me-ow,
    We smell *a rat close by.*

Sing a song of sixpence,
A pocket full of rye;
Four and twenty blackbirds
Baked in a pie.

When the pie was opened,
The birds began to sing;
Was not that a dainty dish
To set before the king?

The king was in his counting-house,
Counting out his money;
The queen was in the parlour,
Eating bread and honey.

The maid was in the garden,
Hanging out the clothes,
When down came a blackbird
And pecked off her nose.

P at a cake, pat a cake, baker's man,
Bake me a cake as fast as you can.
Pat it and prick it, and mark it with B,
And put it in the oven for Baby and me.

S ippity sup, sippity sup,
Bread and milk from a china cup,
Bread and milk from a bright silver spoon,
Made of a piece of the bright silver moon!
Sippity sup, sippity sup,
Sippity, sippity sup!

D ance to your daddy,
My little babby,
Dance to your daddy, my little lamb;
You shall have a fishy
In a little dishy,
You shall have a fishy when the boat comes in.

I will build you a house
  If you do not cry,
A house, little girl,
As tall as the sky.

I will build you a house
Of golden dates,
The freshest of all
For the steps and gates.

I will furnish the house
For you and for me
With walnuts and hazels
Fresh from the tree.

I will build you a house
And when it is done
I will roof it with grapes
To keep out the sun.

Rose Fyleman

Little Boy Blue,
  Come blow your horn,
The sheep's in the meadow,
  The cow's in the corn;
But where is the boy
  Who looks after the sheep?
He's under the haycock,
  Fast asleep.
Will you wake him?
  No, not I,
For if I do,
  He's sure to cry.

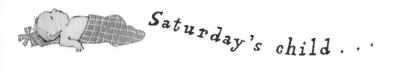

H ush, little baby, don't say a word,
Papa's going to buy you a mockingbird.

If the mockingbird won't sing,
Papa's going to buy you a diamond ring.

If the diamond ring turns to brass,
Papa's going to buy you a looking-glass.

If the looking-glass gets broke,
Papa's going to buy you a billy goat.

If the billy goat runs away,
Papa's going to buy you another today.

The heaven is bright,
The earth is bright,
I have a baby who cries all night.

Thula, thula, mtwana,
Thula, thula, sana,
Thula, thula, baba,
Ubaba, uzofika kusasa,
Thula mtwana.

Zulu Traditional

What are we gonna do with the baby-o?
What are we gonna do with the baby-o?
What are we gonna do with the baby-o?
Whoop him up and let him go.
Prettiest little baby in the country-o
Mammy and pappy both say it's so.
What are we gonna do with the baby-o?
Send him off to sleepy-o.

Sleep brings pearl necklaces, do not cry, baby,
Sleep brings sweet dishes, do not cry, baby,
Do not cry, baby,
It is time, you must sleep now,
As the fish sleeps in the pool.

23

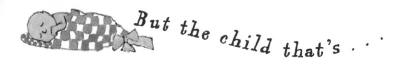

Hush, the waves are rolling in,
    White with foam, white with foam,
Father toils amid the din,
    While baby sleeps at home.

Hush, the ship rides in the gale,
    Where they roam, where they roam,
Father seeks the roving whale,
    While baby sleeps at home.

Hush the wind sweeps o'er the deep,
    All alone, all alone,
Mother now the watch will keep,
    Till father's ship comes home.

Rock-a-bye baby, on the tree top,
When the wind blows, the cradle will rock,
When the bough breaks, the cradle will fall,
Down will come baby, cradle and all.

Rock-a-bye baby, your cradle is green,
Father's a king and mother's a queen,
Betty's a lady and wears a gold ring,
Johnnie's a drummer and drums for the king.

Catch him crow, catch him kite!
Take him away till the apples are ripe,
When the apples are ripe and ready to fall,
Down comes baby, apples and all.

O, my luve is like a red, red rose,
    That's newly sprung in June:
O, my luve is like the melodie
    That's sweetly played in tune.

As fair art thou, my bonnie lass,
    So deep in luve am I;
And I will luve thee still, my dear,
    Till a' the seas gang dry.

Till a' the seas gang dry, my dear,
    And the rocks melt wi' the sun:
And I will luve thee still, my dear,
    While the sands o' life shall run.

And fare thee weel, my only luve,
    And fare thee weel a while!
And I will come again, my luve,
    Tho' it were ten thousand mile!

Robert Burns

28

Lavender's blue, dilly, dilly,
Lavender's green;
When I am king, dilly, dilly,
You shall be queen.

Who told you so, dilly, dilly,
Who told you so?
'Twas mine own heart, dilly, dilly,
That told me so.

Call up your men, dilly, dilly,
Set them to work,
Some to the plough, dilly, dilly,
Some to the fork.

Some to make hay, dilly, dilly,
Some to reap corn,
Whilst you and I, dilly, dilly,
Keep ourselves warm.

Roses are red, dilly, dilly,
Violets are blue;
Because you love me, dilly, dilly,
I will love you.

B ye, baby bunting,
Daddy's gone-a-hunting
Gone to get a rabbit skin
To wrap the baby bunting in.

Toddler Time

Oh, the grand old Duke of York,
    He had ten thousand men,
He marched them up to the top of the hill,
    And he marched them down again.
And when they were up they were up,
    And when they were down they were down,
And when they were only half way up,
    They were neither up nor down.

BOW-WOW, ME-OW-ME-OW, GRUNT-GRUNT, SQUEAK,

One, two, three,
The bumble-bee,
The rooster crows
And away he goes.

TU-WHU, CAW-CAW, QUACK-QUACK, MOO-OO!

D own at the station, early every morning,
Two little puff-puffs, all in a row.
Man on the engine, turns a little handle,
Chuff-chuff-chuff, and away we go!
Chuff-chuff-chuffchuff,
Chuff-chuff-chuffchuff,

33

Hickety, pickety, my black hen,
    She lays eggs for gentlemen;
Gentlemen come every day
To see what my black hen doth lay.

Chop, chop, choppity-chop,
    Cut off the bottom
And cut off the top,
What there is left we will
Put in the pot,
Chop, chop, choppity-chop.

I scream, you scream
We all scream
For ice-cream!

Pease porridge hot,
    Pease porridge cold,
Pease porridge in the pot,
Nine days old.
Some like it hot,
Some like it cold,
Some like it in the pot
Nine days old.

T wo little mice went tripping down the street,
    Pum catta-pum chin chin,
One wore a bonnet and a green silk skirt,
One wore trousers and a nice clean shirt;
Pum catta-pum chin chin.

One little hen went tripping down the street,
Pum catta-pum chin chin,
One little hen very smart and spry,
With a wig-wagging tail and a wicked little eye,
Pum catta-pum chin chin.

Rose Fyleman

J ack be nimble,
    Jack be quick,
Jack jump over
      The candlestick.

L eg over leg
    As the dog went to Dover,
    When he came to a stile
    Jump, he went over.

DOVER

When I was a little boy,
 I washed my mother's dishes.
I put my finger in my ear,
And pulled out little fishes.

Tweedledum
 And Tweedledee
Agreed to have a battle,
For Tweedledum said Tweedledee
Had spoiled his nice new rattle.
Just then flew by a monstrous crow
As big as a tar barrel,
Which frightened both
The heroes so
They quite forgot
Their quarrel.

Georgie Porgie,
 Pudding and pie,
Kissed the girls and made them cry;
When the boys came out to play,
Georgie Porgie ran away.

Little Jack Horner
Sat in a corner
Eating a Christmas pie;
He put in his thumb
And pulled out a plum
And said,

What a good boy am I.

There was a little girl,
And she had a little curl
Right in the middle of her forehead;
When she was good,
She was very, very good,
But when she was bad,
She was horrid.

Here am I,
Little Jumping Joan;
When nobody's with me
I'm all alone.

Little Miss Tuckett
Sat on a bucket,
Eating some peaches and cream;
There came a grasshopper
And tried hard to stop her;
But she said, Go away, or I'll scream.

Little Betty Blue
Lost her holiday shoe:
What can little Betty do?
Give her another to match the other,
And then she may walk out in two.

TU-WHU says the owl,

J ack and Jill went up the hill
To fetch a pail of water;
Jack fell down and broke his crown,
And Jill came tumbling after.

CAW-CAW goes the crow,

Humpty Dumpty sat on a wall,
Humpty Dumpty had a great fall;
All the king's horses,
And all the king's men,
Couldn't put Humpty together again.

Ride a cock-horse to Banbury Cross,
To see a fine lady upon a white horse;
With rings on her fingers and bells on her toes,
She shall have music wherever she goes.

QUACK-QUACK goes the duck,

Twee tweedle dee

Twee tweedle dee

Twee tweedle dee

Old King Cole
   Was a merry old soul,
And a merry old soul was he;
   He called for his pipe,
And he called for his bowl,
   And he called for his fiddlers three.

Now every fiddler, he had a fiddle,
   And a very fine fiddle had he;
Twee tweedle dee, tweedle dee, went the fiddlers.
   Oh, there's none so rare,
As can compare
   With King Cole and his fiddlers three!

And **MOO-OO** says the cow.

I had a little nut tree,
　Nothing would it bear
But a silver nutmeg
　And a golden pear;
The king of Spain's daughter
　Came to visit me,
And all for the sake
　Of my little nut tree.

Pretty maid, pretty maid,
　Where have you been?
Gathering a posy
　To give to the queen.
Pretty maid, pretty maid,
　What gave she you?
She gave me a diamond
　As big as my shoe.

Flying-man, Flying-man,
    Up in the sky,
Where are you going to,
Flying so high?

Over the mountains
And over the sea,
Flying-man, Flying-man,
Can't you take me?

It's raining, it's raining,
    There's a pepper in the box,
And all the little ladies
Are holding up their frocks.

Rain, rain go away,
Come again another day,
Little Johnny wants to play.

Doctor Foster
    Went to Gloucester
In a shower of rain;
He stepped in a puddle,
    Right up to his middle,
And never went there again.

I had a cat and the cat pleased me,
  I fed my cat by yonder tree;
  Cat goes fiddle-i-fee.

I had a hen and the hen pleased me,
I fed my hen by yonder tree;
      Hen goes chimmy-chuck, chimmy-chuck,
      Cat goes fiddle-i-fee.

I had a duck and the duck pleased me,
I fed my duck by yonder tree;
      Duck goes quack, quack,
      Hen goes chimmy-chuck, chimmy-chuck,
      Cat goes fiddle-i-fee.

I had a goose and the goose pleased me,
I fed my goose by yonder tree;
      Goose goes swishy, swashy,
      Duck goes quack, quack,
      Hen goes chimmy-chuck, chimmy-chuck,
      Cat goes fiddle-i-fee.

I had a sheep and the sheep pleased me,
I fed my sheep by yonder tree;
      Sheep goes baa, baa,
      Goose goes swishy, swashy,
      Duck goes quack, quack,
      Hen goes chimmy-chuck, chimmy-chuck,
      Cat goes fiddle-i-fee.

Come, let's to bed
    Says Sleepy-head;
Sit up awhile, says Slow;
Hang on the pot,
Says Greedy-gut,
We'll sup before we go.

To bed, to bed,
Cried Sleepy-head,
But all the rest said No!
It is morning now,
You must milk the cow,
And tomorrow to bed we go.

Blow the fire and make the toast,
    Put the muffins down to roast,
Blow the fire and make the toast,
We'll all have tea.

To bed!

46

R ub-a-dub-dub,
    Three men in a tub,
And who do you think they be?
The butcher, the baker,
The candlestick-maker,
Turn 'em out, knaves all three.

I saw you in the orchard,
I saw you in the sea,
I saw you in the bathtub,
Whoops! Pardon me.

T his little pig had a rub-a-dub,
    This little pig had a scrub-a-scrub,
This little pig-a-wig called out, Bears!
Down came the jar with a loud Slam! Slam!
And this little pig had all the jam.

BEARS!

47

Goosey, goosey gander,
    Wither shall I wander?
Upstairs and downstairs
And in my lady's chamber.

There I met an old man
Who would not say his prayers.
I took him by the left leg
And threw him down the stairs.

Hickory, dickory dock,
    The mouse ran up the clock,
The clock struck one,
    The mouse ran down,
Hickory, dickory dock.

There was an old woman
    Who lived in a shoe,
She had so many children
    She didn't know what to do.
She gave them some broth
    Without any bread;
She whipped them all soundly
    And put them to bed.

Diddle, diddle, dumpling, my son John,
    Went to bed with his trousers on;
    One shoe off, and one shoe on,
    Diddle, diddle, dumpling, my son John.

Wee Willie Winkie runs through the town,
    Upstairs and downstairs in his nightgown,
    Rapping at the window,
    Crying through the lock,
    Are the children in their beds,
    For now it's eight o'clock?

All the chi chi birds they sing till dawn.
  When the daylight comes all the birds are gone.
Chi, chi, chi, chi, chi, chi, what a pretty song.
That is what the birds are singing all night long.

Bam chi chi bam, they sing-a this song,
Bam chi chi bam, sing all the night long.
Bam chi chi bam, then just before the day,
Bam chi chi bam, they fly away.

50

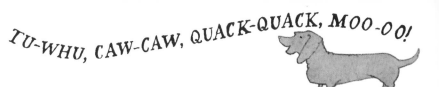

Listen to the tree bear
    Crying in the night
Crying for his mammy
In the pale moonlight.

What will his mammy do
When she hears him cry?
She'll tuck him in a cocoa-pod
And sing a lullaby.

Up the wooden hill
    To Bedfordshire,
Down Sheet Lane
To Blanket Fair.

In the Schoolyard

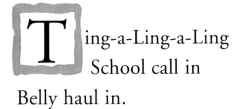 ing-a-Ling-a-Ling
School call in
Belly haul in.

Ting-a-Ling-a-Ling
School over
Belly turn over.

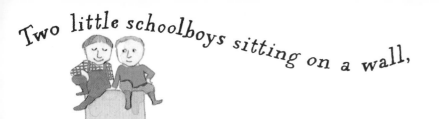 Two little schoolboys sitting on a wall,

Elsie Marley is grown so fine,
 She won't get up to feed the swine,
But lies in bed till eight or nine.
Lazy Elsie Marley.

Frère Jacques, Frère Jacques,
 Dormez-vous? Dormez-vous?
Sonnez les matines! Sonnez les matines!
Ding! Dang! Dong!
Ding! Dang! Dong!

French Traditional

Come, butter, come,
Come, butter, come,
Peter stands at the gate,
Waiting for the butter cake,
Come, butter, come.

I do not like thee, Dr Fell,
The reason why I cannot tell;
But this I know, and know full well,
I do not like thee, Dr Fell.

One misty, moisty morning,
    When cloudy was the weather,
I met a little old man
    Clothed all in leather.

He began to compliment,
    And I began to grin,
How do you do, and how do you do,
    And how do you do again?

Who has seen the wind?
    Neither I nor you;
But when the leaves hang trembling
    The wind is passing thro'.

Who has seen the wind?
    Neither you nor I;
But when the trees bow down their heads
    The wind is passing by.

Christina Rossetti

Here we go round the mulberry bush,
The mulberry bush, the mulberry bush,
Here we go round the mulberry bush,
On a cold and frosty morning.

This is the way we wash our clothes,
Wash our clothes, wash our clothes,
This is the way we wash our clothes,
On a cold and frosty morning.

This is the way we clap our hands,
Clap our hands, clap our hands,
This is the way we clap our hands,
On a cold and frosty morning.

This is the way we go to school,
Go to school, go to school,
This is the way we go to school,
On a cold and frosty morning.

I'm the king of the castle,

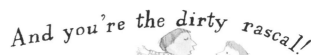

A was an apple pie

B bit it

C cut it

D dealt it

E eat it

F fought for it

G got it

H had it

I inspected it

J joined it

K kept it

L longed for it

M mourned for it

N nodded at it

O opened it

P peeped in it

Q quartered it

R ran for it

S stole it

T took it

U upset it

V viewed it

W wanted it

XYZ & ampersand

All wished for

A piece in hand.

59

Call me this, call me that,

T his is the house that Jack built.

 This is the malt that lay in the house that Jack built.

This is the rat that ate the malt that lay in the house that Jack built.

 This is the cat that killed the rat that ate the malt that lay in the house that Jack built.

This is the dog that worried the cat that killed the rat that ate the malt that lay in the house that Jack built.

This is the cow with the crumpled horn that tossed the dog that worried the cat that killed the rat that ate the malt that lay in the house that Jack built.

This is the maiden all forlorn that milked the cow with the crumpled horn that tossed the dog that worried the cat that killed the rat that ate the malt that lay in the house that Jack built.

This is the man all tattered and torn
that kissed the maiden all forlorn
that milked the cow with the crumpled horn
that tossed the dog that worried the cat
that killed the rat that ate the malt
that lay in the house that Jack built.

This is the priest all shaven and shorn
that married the man all tattered and torn
that kissed the maiden all forlorn
that milked the cow with the crumpled horn
that tossed the dog that worried the cat
that killed the rat that ate the malt
that lay in the house that Jack built.

This is the cock that crowed in the morn that waked the priest all shaven and shorn
that married the man all tattered and torn that kissed the maiden all forlorn
that milked the cow with the crumpled horn that tossed the dog
that worried the cat that killed the rat that ate the malt
that lay in the house that Jack built.

This is the farmer sowing his corn that kept the cock that crowed in the morn
that waked the priest all shaven and shorn that married the man all tattered and torn
that kissed the maiden all forlorn that milked the cow with the crumpled horn
that tossed the dog that worried the cat
that killed the rat that ate the malt
that lay in the house that Jack built.

Sticks and stones will break my bones,

Round and round and round she goes,
And where she stops, nobody knows.
Point to the east, point to the west,
Point to the one that you love the best.

Onesies, twosies,
roundabout, to-backsies.

One potato, two potato,
Three potatoes, four,
Five potatoes, six potatoes,
Seven potatoes more.

There was a farmer who had a dog,
And Bingo was his name-o.
B-I-N-G-O, B-I-N-G-O, B-I-N-G-O,
And Bingo was his name-o.

and Bingo was his name-o.

Ring-a-ring o'roses,
A pocket full of posies.
A-tishoo! A-tishoo!
We all fall down.

We push, we pull
To saw up the wood.
We make a fine house.
It has to be good
To keep a sweet spouse.

Step on a crack,
You'll break your mother's back.
Step on a line,
You'll break your father's spine.

63

Red, white and blue, I'll chase you!

The Queen of Hearts
    She made some tarts,
        All on a summer's day;
The Knave of Hearts
He stole the tarts,
        And took them clean away.

The King of Hearts
Called for the tarts,
        And beat the Knave full sore;
The Knave of Hearts
Brought back the tarts
        And vowed he'd steal no more.

Old Mother Hubbard
Went to the cupboard,
To fetch her poor dog a bone;
But when she got there
The cupboard was bare
And so the poor dog had none.

She went to the baker's
To buy him some bread;
But when she came back
The poor dog was dead.

She went to the tailor's
To buy him a coat;
But when she came back
He was riding a goat.

She went to the undertaker's
To buy him a coffin;
But when she came back
The poor dog was laughing.

She went to the barber's
To buy him a wig;
But when she came back
He was dancing a jig.

She went to the tavern
For white wine and red;
But when she came back
The dog stood on his head.

The dame made a curtsey,
The dog made a bow;
The dame said, Your servant,
The dog said, Bow-wow.

She went to the fruiterer's
To buy him some fruit;
But when she came back
He was playing the flute.

Bow-wow

65

One, two,
Buckle my shoe;
Three, four,
Knock at the door;
Five, six,
Pick up sticks;
Seven, eight,
Lay them straight;
Nine, ten,
A big fat hen;
Eleven, twelve,
Dig and delve;
Thirteen, fourteen,
Maids a-courting;
Fifteen, sixteen,
Maids in the kitchen;
Seventeen, eighteen,
Maids in waiting;
Nineteen, twenty,
My plate's empty.

Un, deux, trois, j'irai dans le bois,
    Quatre, cinq, six, chercher les cerises,
Sept, huit, neuf, dans mon panier neuf,
Dix, onze, douze, elles seront toutes rouges.

French Traditional

Baa, baa, black sheep,
    Have you any wool?
Yes, sir, yes, sir,
Three bags full;
One for the master,
And one for the dame,
And one for the little boy
Who lives down the lane.

Chook, chook, chook, chook, chook,
    Good Morning, Mrs Hen,
How many chickens have you got?
Madam, I've got ten.
Four of them are yellow,
And four of them are brown,
And two of them are speckled red,
The nicest in the town.

The monkey thought it was all in fun,

Mary had a little lamb,
    Its fleece was white as snow;
And everywhere that Mary went
    The lamb was sure to go.

It followed her to school one day,
    That was against the rule;
It made the children laugh and play
    To see a lamb in school.

And so the teacher turned it out,
    But still it lingered near;
And waited patiently about
    Till Mary did appear.

Why does the lamb love Mary so?
    The eager children cry;
Why, Mary loves the lamb, you know,
    The teacher did reply.

Girls and boys
    Come out to play,
The moon is shining
    Bright as day;

Leave your supper,
    And leave your sleep,
And come with your playfellows
    Into the street;

Come with a whoop,
    And come with a call,
Come with a good will,
    Or come not at all,

Come let us dance
    On the open green,
And she who holds longest
    Shall be our queen.

Two little school-friends sitting on the wall,

Ladies and gentlemen,
  Children, too,
Us two chicks gonna boogy for you,
Gonna turn around,
Touch the ground,
And shimmy, shimmy, shimmy
All around.
I don't like college,
I don't like school,
But when it comes to boogyin',
I'm an alligatin' fool . . .

Shimmy Shimmy

70

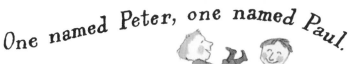

Ahorse and a flea and three blind mice
Sat on a curbstone shooting dice,
The horse said 'Oops!' and fell on the flea,
And the flea said, 'Whoops, there's a horse on me!'

Boom, boom, ain't it great to be crazy,
Boom, boom, ain't it great to be crazy,
To be silly and foolish the whole day through,
Boom, boom, ain't it great to be crazy.

Way down south where the bananas grow,
An ant stepped on an elephant's toe,
The elephant cried with tears in his eyes,
'Why don't you pick on someone your size?'

Boom

Boom

Boom, boom, ain't it great to be crazy . . .

No more licks No more Latin
    To make me cry No more French
No more eyewater No more sitting
To come out of my eye. On de old school bench.

All Join In

G iddyap, horsie, to the fair.
What'll we buy when we get there?
A penny apple and a penny pear.
Giddyap, horsie, to the fair.

This is the key of the kingdom.

Hot cross buns!
  Hot cross buns!
One a penny, two a penny,
Hot cross buns!

If you have no daughters,
Give them to your sons;
One a penny, two a penny,
Hot cross buns!

Smiling girls, rosy boys,
  Come and buy my little toys,
Monkeys made of gingerbread,
And sugar horses painted red.

To market, to market,
To buy a fat pig,
Home again, home again
Jiggety-jig.

Simple Simon met a pieman,
Going to the fair;
Says Simple Simon to the pieman,
Let me taste your ware.

Says the pieman to Simple Simon,
Show me first your penny;
Says Simple Simon to the pieman,
Indeed I have not any.

75

O dear, what can the matter be?
Dear, dear, what can the matter be?
O dear, what can the matter be?
Johnny's so long at the fair.

He promised he'd buy me a fairing should please me,
And then for a kiss, oh! he vowed he would tease me,
He promised he'd bring me a bunch of blue ribbons
To tie up my bonny brown hair.

Friday night's dream
　　On the Saturday told,
Is sure to come true,
Be it ever so old.

Those dressed in blue
　　Have loves true;
In green and white,
Forsaken quite.

Somebody loves you
　　Deep and true.
If I weren't so shy,
I'd tell you who.

Red stockings, blue stockings,
　　Shoes tied up with silver;
A red rosette upon my breast
And a gold ring on my finger.

Choose your partner, skip to my Lou,
Choose your partner, skip to my Lou,
Choose your partner, skip to my Lou,
Skip to my Lou, my darling.

Lou, Lou, skip to my Lou,
Lou, Lou, skip to my Lou,
Lou, Lou, skip to my Lou,
Skip to my Lou, my darling.

(REPEAT AFTER EACH VERSE)

Chickens in the garden, shoo, shoo, shoo,
Chickens in the garden, shoo, shoo, shoo,
Chickens in the garden, shoo, shoo, shoo,
Skip to my Lou, my darling.

Cow in the kitchen, moo, cow, moo,
Cow in the kitchen, moo, cow, moo,
Cow in the kitchen, moo, cow, moo,
Skip to my Lou, my darling.

Hogs in the potato patch, rooting up corn,
Hogs in the potato patch, rooting up corn,
Hogs in the potato patch, rooting up corn,
Skip to my Lou, my darling.

Going to the market, two by two,
Going to the market, two by two,
Going to the market, two by two,
Skip to my Lou, my darling.

Back from market, what did you do?
Back from market, what did you do?
Back from market, what did you do?
Skip to my Lou, my darling.

Had a glass of buttermilk, one and two,
Had a glass of buttermilk, one and two,
Had a glass of buttermilk, one and two,
Skip to my Lou, my darling.

Flies in the sugar bowl, shoo, fly, shoo!
Flies in the sugar bowl, shoo, fly, shoo!
Flies in the sugar bowl, shoo, fly, shoo!
Skip to my Lou, my darling.

Lou, Lou, skip to my Lou... Lou, Lou, skip to my Lou...

 In that house there waits a room,

She'll be coming round the mountain, when she comes (Yee, ha!),
   She'll be coming round the mountain, when she comes (Yee, ha!),
She'll be coming round the mountain,
Coming round the mountain,
Coming round the mountain, when she comes (Yee, ha!).

Yee, ha!

In that room there is a bed,

(FIRST LINES OF FURTHER VERSES)

She'll be driving six white horses, when she comes . . . Whoa, back!

Oh, we'll all go out to meet her, when she comes . . . Hi, babe!

Oh, we'll kill the old red rooster, when she comes . . . Cock-a-doodle-doo!

And we'll all have chicken and dumplings, when she comes . . . Yum, yum!

Oh, she'll have to sleep with grandma, when she comes . . . Snore, snore!

And she'll be wearing pink pyjamas, when she comes . . . Whee-whoooooooooo!

On that bed there is a basket

Merry are the bells, and merry would they ring,
  Merry was myself, and merry would I sing;
With a merry ding-dong, happy, gay and free,
And a merry sing-song, happy let us be!

U p in the green orchard there is a green tree,
The finest of pippins that you may see;
The apples are ripe, and ready to fall,
And Robin and Richard shall gather them all.

T he boughs do shake and the bells do ring,
So merrily comes our harvest in,
Our harvest in, our harvest in,
So merrily comes our harvest in.

We've ploughed, we've sowed,
We've reaped, we've mowed,
We've got our harvest in.

Flowers, basket, basket on the bed,

Peter Piper picked a peck of pickled pepper;
    A peck of pickled pepper Peter Piper picked.
If Peter Piper picked a peck of pickled pepper,
Where's the peck of pickled pepper Peter Piper picked?

She sells sea-shells on the sea shore;
    The shells that she sells are sea-shells I'm sure.
So if she sells sea-shells on the sea shore,
I'm sure that the shells are sea-shore shells.

Swan swam over the sea,
    Swim, swan, swim!
Swan swam back again,
Well swum, swan!

Three grey geese in a green field grazing,
    Grey were the geese and green was the grazing.

I t stays all year,
But it leaves in the spring.
It has a bark,
But it doesn't sing.

W ith a million pennies
On a golden fan,
Who is richer
Than the richest man?

W ithout a bridle or a saddle,
Across a thing I ride and straddle,
And those I ride, by the help of me,
Though almost blind are made to see.

T wo brothers we are,
Great burdens we bear,
On which we are bitterly pressed;
The truth is to say,
We are full all the day,
And empty when we go to rest.

Cock-a-doodle-doo!

A bright red flower he wears on his head;
His beautiful coat needs no thimble nor thread;
And though he's not fearsome, I'll have you know,
Ten thousand doors open when he says so!

Ladies and Jellypots,
  I come before you, not behind you,
To tell you something I know nothing about.
I went to the show tomorrow,
And took a front seat at the back.
I fell from the floor to the gallery,
And hurt the front of my back.
The man at the door was shouting:
'Admission free, pay at the door.'

It was midnight on the ocean,
  Not a street car was in sight.
The sun was shining brightly,
  And it rained all day that night.

A barefoot boy with shoes on
  Came shuffling down the street,
His pants were full of pockets,
  His shoes were full of feet.

A flea and a fly in a flue
Were caught, so what could they do?
　　Said the fly, 'Let us flee.'
　　'Let us fly,' said the flea.
So they flew through a flaw in the flue.

T here once were two cats of Kilkenny,
Each thought there was one cat too many;
　　So they fought and they fit,
　　And they scratched and they bit,
Till instead of two cats there weren't any.

T here was an old man from Peru
Who dreamed he was eating a shoe.
　　He woke in a fright
　　In the middle of the night,
　　And found it was perfectly true.

A diner while dining at Crewe
Found quite a large mouse in his stew.
　　Said the waiter, 'Don't shout,
　　And wave it about,
Or the rest will be wanting one, too.'

There was an old woman tossed up in a basket,
   Seventeen times as high as the moon;
And where she was going, I couldn't but ask it,
   For in her hand she carried a broom.

'Old woman, old woman, old woman,' quoth I,
   'O whither, O whither, O whither, so high?'
'To brush the cobwebs off the sky!'
      'Shall I go with thee?'
      'Ay, by-and-by.'

Hey diddle diddle,
  The cat and the fiddle,
  The cow jumped over the moon;
The little dog laughed
To see such sport,
  And the dish ran away with the spoon.

The Owl and the Pussy-Cat went to sea
   In a beautiful pea-green boat,
They took some honey, and plenty of money,
   Wrapped in a five-pound note.
The Owl looked up to the stars above,
   And sang to a small guitar,
'O lovely Pussy, O Pussy, my love,
   What a beautiful Pussy you are,
      You are,
      You are!
   What a beautiful Pussy you are!'

Pussy said to the Owl, 'You elegant fowl!
   How charmingly sweet you sing!
O! let us be married! too long we have tarried
   But what shall we do for a ring?'
They sailed away, for a year and a day,
   To the land where the Bong-tree grows
And there in a wood a Piggy-wig stood
   With a ring at the end of his nose,
      His nose,
      His nose,
   With a ring at the end of his nose.

'Dear Pig, are you willing to sell for one shilling
    Your ring?' Said the Piggy, 'I will.'
So they took it away, and were married next day
    By the Turkey who lives on the hill.
They dined on mince and slices of quince,
    Which they ate with a runcible spoon;
And hand in hand, on the edge of the sand,
    They danced by the light of the moon,
        The moon,
        The moon,
    They danced by the light of the moon.

Edward Lear

91

It's time, I believe,
For us to get leave:
The little dog says
It isn't, it is, it isn't, it is . . .

INDEX OF TITLES AND FIRST LINES

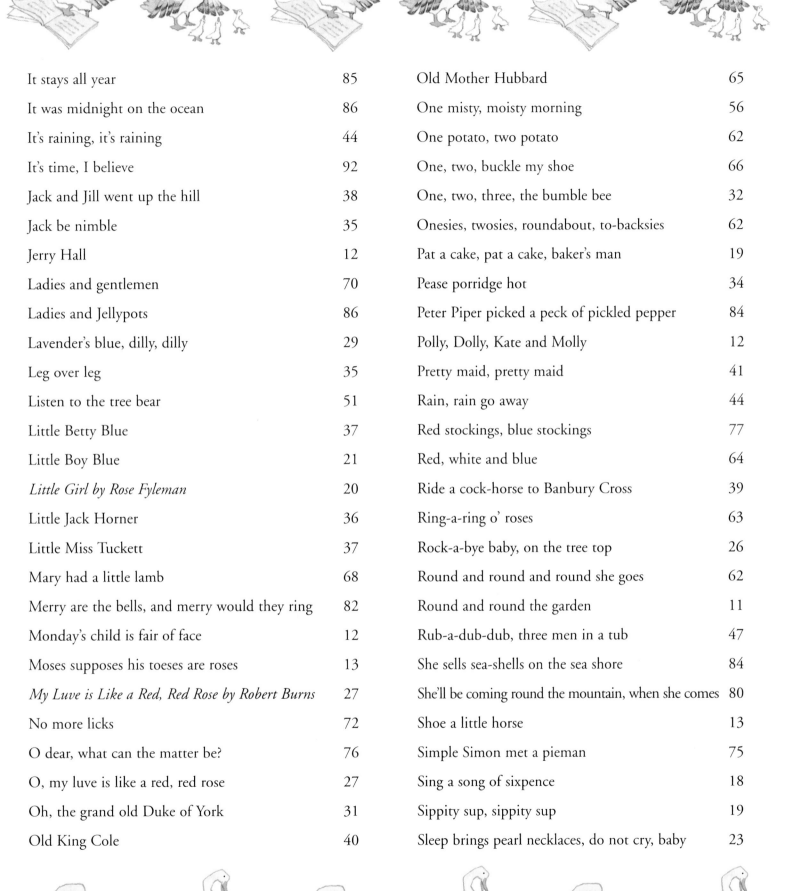

Acknowledgements

The publisher would like to thank the copyright holders for permission to reproduce the following copyright material:

Baby Face: Copyright © 1926; renewed, terminated, and reverted to B&G Akst Music Co. and Benny Davis Music Co.
Rights for the British Reversionary Territories controlled by Memory Lane Music Limited, London. All rights reserved. Reprinted with permission

A Farmyard Song: Extract from *The Oxford Nursery Rhyme Book* edited by Iona and Peter Opie
(Oxford University Press 1955) by permission of Oxford University Press.

It's time, I believe: Extract from *I Saw Esau*. Text © 1992 Iona Opie. Illustrated by Maurice Sendak.
Reproduced by permission of the publisher Walker Books Ltd.

Little Girl and **Well I Never!**: The Society of Authors as the Literary Representative of the Estate of Rose Fyleman.

Every effort has been made to obtain permission to reproduce copyright material
but there may be cases where we have been unable to trace or contact a copyright holder.
The publisher will be happy to rectify any errors or omissions in future printings.